D0651890

⁶⁄₀₄

Brooke County Public Library
945 Main Street
Wellsburg, WV
304-737-1551

DEMCO

STATES

KENTUCKY

A MyReportLinks.com Book

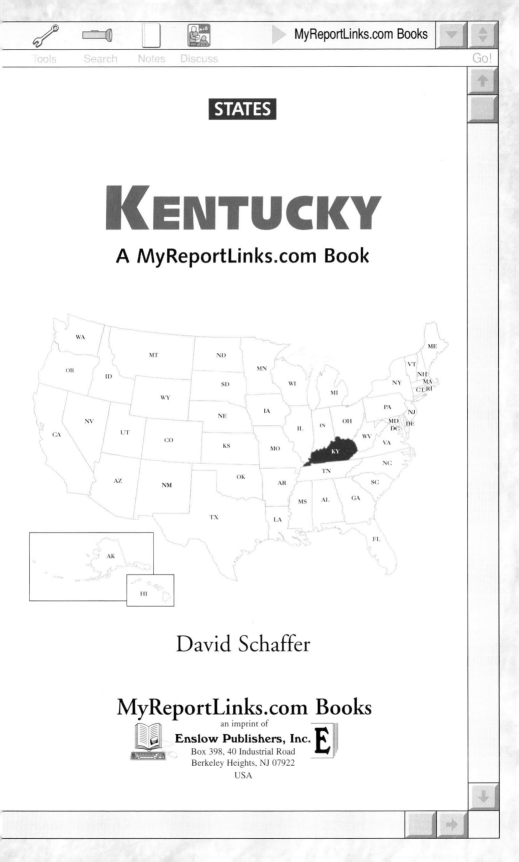

David Schaffer

MyReportLinks.com Books

an imprint of

Enslow Publishers, Inc.

Box 398, 40 Industrial Road
Berkeley Heights, NJ 07922
USA

MyReportLinks.com Books, an imprint of Enslow Publishers, Inc. MyReportLinks is a trademark of Enslow Publishers, Inc.

Library of Congress Cataloging-in-Publication Data

Schaffer, David.
  Kentucky / David Schaffer.
     p. cm. — (States)
Summary: Discusses the land and climate, economy, government, and history of the Bluegrass State. Includes Internet links to Web sites related to Kentucky.
Includes bibliographical references and index.
  ISBN 0-7660-5126-9
  1. Kentucky—Juvenile literature. [1. Kentucky.] I. Title. II.
Series: States (Series : Berkeley Heights, N.J.)
F451.3.S33 2003
976.9—dc21

                           2002014852

Printed in the United States of America

10 9 8 7 6 5 4 3 2 1

To Our Readers:
Through the purchase of this book, you and your library gain access to the Report Links that specifically back up this book.

The Publisher will provide access to the Report Links that back up this book and will keep these Report Links up to date on **www.myreportlinks.com** for three years from the book's first publication date.

We have done our best to make sure all Internet addresses in this book were active and appropriate when we went to press. However, the author and the Publisher have no control over, and assume no liability for, the material available on those Internet sites or on other Web sites they may link to.

The usage of the MyReportLinks.com Books Web site is subject to the terms and conditions stated on the Usage Policy Statement on **www.myreportlinks.com**.

In the future, a password may be required to access the Report Links that back up this book. The password is found on the bottom of page 4 of this book.

Any comments or suggestions can be sent by e-mail to comments@myreportlinks.com or to the address on the back cover.

Photo Credits: Army Knowledge Online, p. 17; *Blazing the Wilderness Road with Daniel Boone in American History.* Chapter 5, p. 43., p. 35; © Corel Corporation, p. 21; © 1995 Photodisc, pp. 11, 28, 41; *Dictionary of American Portraits,* Dover Publications, Inc., © 1967, p. 39; Kentucky Coal Council/Kentucky Coal Association, p. 25; Kentucky Department for Libraries and Archives, p. 42; Kentucky Educational Television, p. 32; Kentucky Department of Tourism, p. 20; Kentucky State Legislature, p. 31; Kentucky State Nature Preserves Commission, p. 19; Kentucky State Parks, p. 44; KFC Corporation, p. 16; Library of Congress, p. 27; Library of Congress Bicentennial, p. 33; Roughstock Productions, p. 13; The U.S. House of Representatives Office of the Clerk, p. 37; *Time* Magazine, p. 15; University of Kentucky, p. 29; White House, p. 38.

Cover Photo: Gene Burch

Cover Description: Kentucky State Capitol Building

Contents

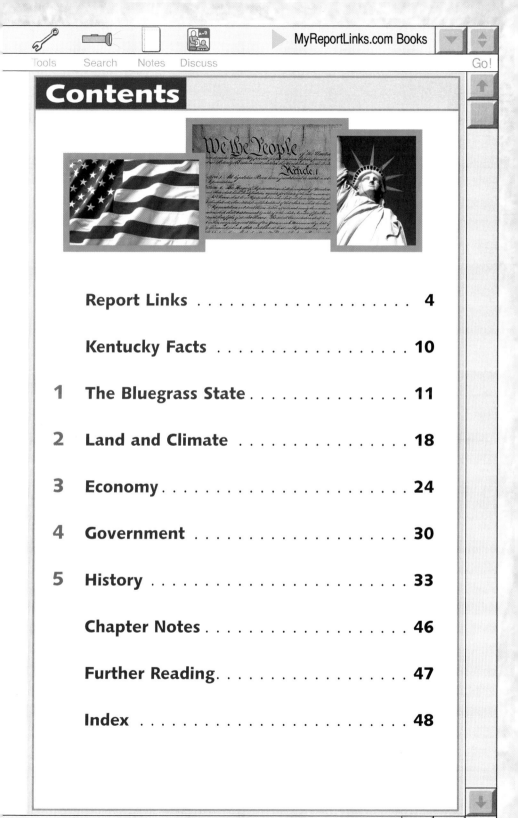

MyReportLinks.com Books
Great Books, Great Links, Great for Research!

MyReportLinks.com Books present the information you need to learn about your report subject. In addition, they show you where to go on the Internet for more information. The pre-evaluated Report Links that back up this book are kept up to date on **www.myreportlinks.com**. With the purchase of a MyReportLinks.com Books title, you and your library gain access to the Report Links that specifically back up that book. The Report Links save hours of research time and link to dozens—even hundreds—of Web sites, source documents, and photos related to your report topic.

Please see "To Our Readers" on the Copyright page for important information about this book, the MyReportLinks.com Books Web site, and the Report Links that back up this book.

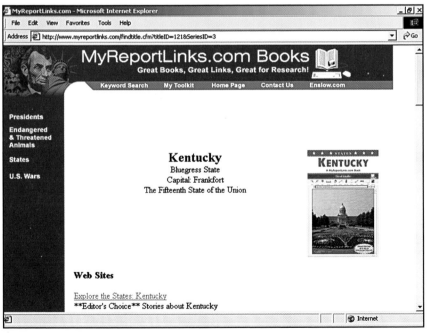

Access:

The Publisher will provide access to the Report Links that back up this book and will try to keep these Report Links up to date on our Web site for three years from the book's first publication date. Please enter **SKY1596** if asked for a password.

Report Links

The Internet sites described below can be accessed at http://www.myreportlinks.com

*EDITOR'S CHOICE

▶ **Explore the States: Kentucky**
America's Story from America's Library, a Library of Congress Web site, tells the story of Kentucky. Here you will find stories about the Kentucky Derby, the Trail of Tears, and the Trigg County Country Ham Festival.

Link to this Internet site from http://www.myreportlinks.com

*EDITOR'S CHOICE

▶ *World Almanac for Kids Online:* **Kentucky**
The *World Almanac for Kids Online* provides facts and statistics about Kentucky. Here you can view population tables and learn about the land and resources, government and politics, and history.

Link to this Internet site from http://www.myreportlinks.com

*EDITOR'S CHOICE

▶ **Living the Story: The Civil Rights Movement in Kentucky**
Living the Story: The Civil Rights Movement in Kentucky allows visitors to read biographies of those involved in the movement, and view an image gallery and a time line of events.

Link to this Internet site from http://www.myreportlinks.com

*EDITOR'S CHOICE

▶ **Local Legacies: Kentucky**
The Library of Congress Web site explores local legacies in Kentucky. These include the Kentucky Derby Festival, Tater Day Festival, and many others.

Link to this Internet site from http://www.myreportlinks.com

*EDITOR'S CHOICE

▶ **Kentucky**
Infoplease.com provides a brief overview of Kentucky and its history. You will also find links to profiles of famous Kentucky natives and residents.

Link to this Internet site from http://www.myreportlinks.com

*EDITOR'S CHOICE

▶ **Internet Public Library: Kentucky**
Kidsplace @ The Internet Public Library presents facts and statistics about Kentucky. You will also find a "Did you Know . . ." section with interesting facts about Kentucky and links to almanacs and encyclopedias with additional information about the state.

Link to this Internet site from http://www.myreportlinks.com

Any comments? Contact us: **comments@myreportlinks.com**   5

Report Links

The Internet sites described below can be accessed at
http://www.myreportlinks.com

▶**Abraham Lincoln's Birthplace**
The National Park Service Web site provides a brief description of Abraham Lincoln's birthplace, located near Hodgenville, Kentucky. Click on "InDepth" to learn more about the park.

Link to this Internet site from http://www.myreportlinks.com

▶**Bill Monroe and Bluegrass**
In 1970, Kentuckian Bill Monroe was elected to the Country Music Hall of Fame. This Web site provides a brief overview of his life and music career.

Link to this Internet site from http://www.myreportlinks.com

▶**CivilWar@Smithsonian**
By navigating through the CivilWar@Smithsonian Web site you can explore Kentucky's role in the Civil War and learn about influential Kentuckians.

Link to this Internet site from http://www.myreportlinks.com

▶**Colonel Harland Sanders**
The KFC Web site provides a brief history of the franchise as well as a biography of Colonel Harland Sanders.

Link to this Internet site from http://www.myreportlinks.com

▶**Cumberland Gap**
The Cumberland Gap is located near Middlesboro, Kentucky. The National Park Service Web site provides a brief overview of the park's history. Click on "InDepth" to learn more.

Link to this Internet site from http://www.myreportlinks.com

▶**Discovering Lewis & Clark**
Did you know that William Clark was from Kentucky? Discovering Lewis & Clark is a comprehensive Web site with information about Lewis and Clark's preparation for the journey, their exploration, and their return trip.

Link to this Internet site from http://www.myreportlinks.com

Report Links

The Internet sites described below can be accessed at
http://www.myreportlinks.com

▶ **Expanding Frontier and Daniel Boone**
This brief article about Daniel Boone discusses how he became perhaps
America's most famous frontiersman.

Link to this Internet site from http://www.myreportlinks.com

▶ **Fort Knox Gold Vault Retains Mystique**
Did you know that it has been said that no one person has the
combination to the vault at Fort Knox? This article discusses some
of the mysteries of the Fort Knox gold vault in Kentucky.

Link to this Internet site from http://www.myreportlinks.com

▶ **If Slavery Is Not Wrong, Nothing Is Wrong**
This brief article discusses a meeting between Abraham Lincoln and
Kentucky representatives, former Senator Archibald Dixon, Governor
Thomas E. Bramlette, and Albert G. Hodges, where they debated the
right of African Americans to serve in the Federal Army.

Link to this Internet site from http://www.myreportlinks.com

▶ *Kentucky Atlas and Gazetteer*
This site provides an interactive atlas of the Commonwealth of
Kentucky. It includes geographical and topographical maps as well
as descriptions of counties, regional features, and characteristics.

Link to this Internet site from http://www.myreportlinks.com

▶ **Kentucky Coal Education Web Site**
The Kentucky Coal Education Web site provides an overview of the
role coal has played in Kentucky's history and economy.

Link to this Internet site from http://www.myreportlinks.com

▶ **Kentucky Derby**
The official site of the Kentucky Derby includes coverage of this year's
Derby as well as extensive historical information.

Link to this Internet site from http://www.myreportlinks.com

Report Links

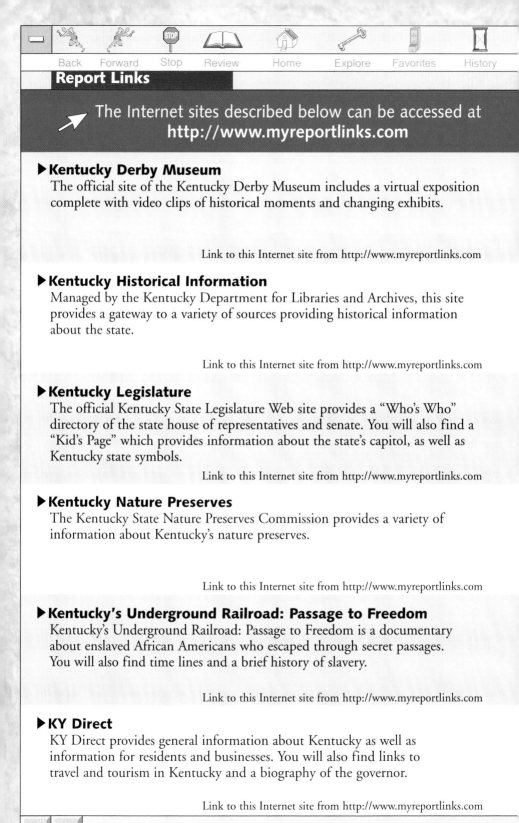

The Internet sites described below can be accessed at
http://www.myreportlinks.com

▶**Kentucky Derby Museum**
The official site of the Kentucky Derby Museum includes a virtual exposition
complete with video clips of historical moments and changing exhibits.

Link to this Internet site from http://www.myreportlinks.com

▶**Kentucky Historical Information**
Managed by the Kentucky Department for Libraries and Archives, this site
provides a gateway to a variety of sources providing historical information
about the state.

Link to this Internet site from http://www.myreportlinks.com

▶**Kentucky Legislature**
The official Kentucky State Legislature Web site provides a "Who's Who"
directory of the state house of representatives and senate. You will also find a
"Kid's Page" which provides information about the state's capitol, as well as
Kentucky state symbols.

Link to this Internet site from http://www.myreportlinks.com

▶**Kentucky Nature Preserves**
The Kentucky State Nature Preserves Commission provides a variety of
information about Kentucky's nature preserves.

Link to this Internet site from http://www.myreportlinks.com

▶**Kentucky's Underground Railroad: Passage to Freedom**
Kentucky's Underground Railroad: Passage to Freedom is a documentary
about enslaved African Americans who escaped through secret passages.
You will also find time lines and a brief history of slavery.

Link to this Internet site from http://www.myreportlinks.com

▶**KY Direct**
KY Direct provides general information about Kentucky as well as
information for residents and businesses. You will also find links to
travel and tourism in Kentucky and a biography of the governor.

Link to this Internet site from http://www.myreportlinks.com

Any comments? Contact us: **comments@myreportlinks.com**

Report Links

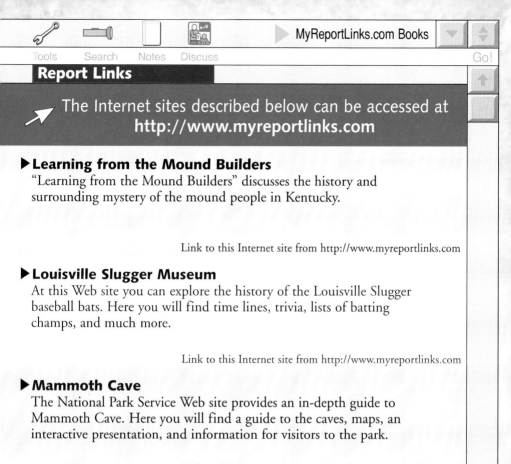

The Internet sites described below can be accessed at
http://www.myreportlinks.com

▶ **Learning from the Mound Builders**
"Learning from the Mound Builders" discusses the history and
surrounding mystery of the mound people in Kentucky.

Link to this Internet site from http://www.myreportlinks.com

▶ **Louisville Slugger Museum**
At this Web site you can explore the history of the Louisville Slugger
baseball bats. Here you will find time lines, trivia, lists of batting
champs, and much more.

Link to this Internet site from http://www.myreportlinks.com

▶ **Mammoth Cave**
The National Park Service Web site provides an in-depth guide to
Mammoth Cave. Here you will find a guide to the caves, maps, an
interactive presentation, and information for visitors to the park.

Link to this Internet site from http://www.myreportlinks.com

▶ **Muhammad Ali**
Muhammad Ali is a native Kentuckian who was voted one of *Time*
magazine's one hundred greatest people of the twentieth century. This
biography of Muhammad Ali discusses his life and career in boxing.

Link to this Internet site from http://www.myreportlinks.com

▶ **Today In History**
This Web site tells the story of Daniel Boone's first sighting of
Kentucky on June 7, 1769.

Link to this Internet site from http://www.myreportlinks.com

▶ **U.S. Census Bureau: Kentucky**
At this Web site you will find the official census statistics on the
state of Kentucky. Learn about the population figures, business facts,
geography facts, and more.

Link to this Internet site from http://www.myreportlinks.com

Capital
Frankfort

Population
4,041,769*

Counties
120

Gained Statehood
June 1, 1792, the fifteenth state

Bird
Kentucky cardinal

Tree
Tulip poplar

Flower
Goldenrod

Wild Animal
Gray squirrel

Horse
Thoroughbred

Dog
Beagle

Fish
Kentucky bass

Butterfly
Viceroy

Mineral
Coal

Gemstone
Freshwater pearl

Song
"My Old Kentucky Home"
(by Stephen Foster)

Motto
United We Stand,
Divided We Fall

Flag
A dark-blue background with the state seal in the center. Two men, a frontiersman and a statesman, are shown shaking hands. The state motto, "United We Stand, Divided We Fall," is printed above and below the two men. A goldenrod wreath decorates the bottom.

Nickname
Bluegrass state

Population reflects the 2000 census.

The Bluegrass State

Kentucky lies in the south-central United States. The state played a key role in the growth and development of the West. In its early days, Kentucky was seen as an almost ideal place. It was even described as a promised land.

Kentucky was also an important state in the Civil War, although few major battles were fought on Kentucky soil. Both Abraham Lincoln and Jefferson Davis—opposing leaders in that war—were born in Kentucky.

▲ In the early twentieth century, the number of Kentuckians living in rural areas decreased from three fourths to less than one half of the total residents.

Until the early twentieth century, three quarters of Kentucky's people lived in rural areas or small towns making agricultural products. Now more than half live in urban areas, and manufacturing has become an important part of the state's economy.

A Symbol of the Western Frontier

Kentucky played a key role in the nation's westward expansion. Hunters, traders, and settlers flocked into the area, and many people passed through on their way to settle farther west.

Stephen A. Channing, an expert on U.S. history, says:

> . . . It was Kentucky that became the focus of the growing appetite for new lands . . . It was Kentucky that witnessed the first important English settlements beyond the mountains. It was Kentucky that channelled the great movement of peoples into the Mississippi Valley. And it was in and of Kentucky that some of the most persistent and characteristic myths of frontier America were shaped.[1]

However, early travelers and settlers in Kentucky often found that their dream of the new frontier did not match reality. Among other hardships, the settlers often clashed with the American Indians in the area.

The Bluegrass State

Kentucky gets its nickname from its most famous natural feature. Bluegrass is actually dark green. However, in spring, the buds of this grass have a bluish tint.

The Bluegrass region of Kentucky is famous for its thoroughbred horses and horse racing. The Kentucky Derby has been held every year in Louisville since 1875. It is the most popular horse race in the country and one of the leading sporting events in the world. The famous horse

Tools　　Search　　Notes　　Discuss　　　　　　　　　　　　　Go!

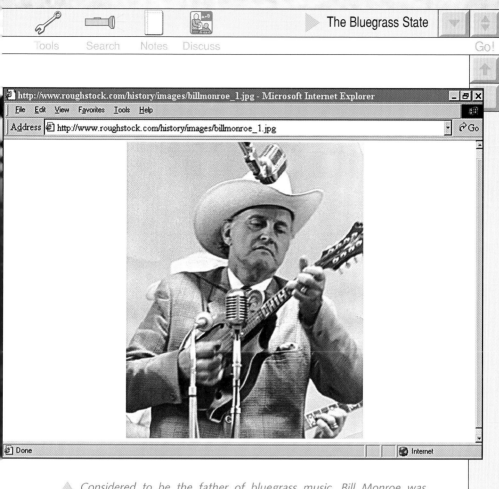

http://www.roughstock.com/history/images/billmonroe_1.jpg - Microsoft Internet Explorer

File　Edit　View　Favorites　Tools　Help

Address http://www.roughstock.com/history/images/billmonroe_1.jpg　　　 Go

Done　　　　　　　　　　　　　　　　　　　　　　　　Internet

▲ *Considered to be the father of bluegrass music, Bill Monroe was the recipient of many honors, including the Grammy Lifetime Achievement Award. His song "Blue Moon of Kentucky" was officially adopted as the official state bluegrass song of Kentucky in 1988.*

Secretariat set a record at the Derby in 1973 that has still not been beaten. Calumet Farm in Kentucky is among those known for breeding winners. Nine Kentucky Derby winners were bred at this farm.

Bluegrass is also the name of a form of music that originated in eastern Kentucky and elsewhere in Southeast Appalachia (the southeastern part of the Appalachian Mountains). The music grew out of traditional mountain folk music and gospel songs, and it combined Scottish, Irish, and African-American influences. Bluegrass is played mainly with stringed instruments such as fiddles, banjos, and mandolins. It often has a fast tempo. Kentucky native Bill Monroe has been called the Father of Bluegrass. He formed a band called the Blue Grass Boys in the late 1930s. Two members of Monroe's band—Lester Flatt and Earl Scruggs—went on to become famous in their own right. The International Bluegrass Music Museum is in Owensboro, Kentucky. Monroe, Flatt, and Scruggs were the first three inductees to its Hall of Honor.

Famous Kentuckians

Many well-known people were born in or residents of Kentucky. Daniel Boone, the legendary frontiersman, is one of the most famous. He explored the area in the 1760s and 1770s, and built a road and a fort there. Henry Clay (1777–1852) represented Kentucky in Congress for many years and ran unsuccessfully for president three times.

Abraham Lincoln, president of the United States during the Civil War, was born in Kentucky. A log cabin like the one he was born in marks his birthplace near the town of Hodgenville. Jefferson Davis, president of the Confederate States during the Civil War, was born in Fairview, Kentucky.

Other Kentuckians have been prominent government and civil leaders. John Cabell Breckinridge (1821–75) was the fourteenth vice president of the United States under President James Buchanan. Alben William Barkley (1877–1956) was the thirty-fifth vice president under President Harry S Truman. Whitney Moore Young, Jr., was the head of the National Urban League and played a major role in getting civil rights laws passed during the 1960s. His father, Whitney Moore Young, Sr., was also a civil rights activist. In 1983, Martha Layne Collins was the first

Leaders & Revolutionaries | Artists & Entertainers | Builders & Titans | Scientists & Thinkers | **Heroes & Icons** | Person of the Century

The Century | Beautiful People | Great Romances | Dubious Influences | Sports Moments

TIME 100 POLLS
The 100
Person of the Century
Event of the Century
Phonies and Frauds
100 Worst Ideas

Emmeline Pankhurst
Helen Keller
Charles Lindbergh
Bill Wilson
American G.I.
Jackie Robinson
Anne Frank
Billy Graham
Edmund Hillary &
Tenzing Norgay
Rosa Parks
Che Guevara
Marilyn Monroe
The Kennedys
Muhammad Ali
Bruce Lee
Pelé
Harvey Milk

The Greatest
Muhammad Ali

Floating, stinging, punching, prophesying, he transformed his sport and became the world's most adored athlete

BY GEORGE PLIMPTON

Oliver Wendell Holmes once observed that every profession is great that is greatly pursued. Boxing in the early 60s, largely controlled by the Mob, was in a moribund state until Muhammad Ali--Cassius Clay, in those days--appeared on the scene. "Just when the sweet science appears to lie like a painted ship upon a painted ocean," wrote A. J. Liebling, "a new Hero comes along

CORBIS/BETTMANN

READ the transcript of TIME's chat with George Plimpton on Muhammad Ali

--> BORN Born
Cassius Clay, Jan.
17, 1942, in

CURRENT ISSUE

Subscribe to TIME

Cover: Bush's Success
Story: G.O.P. Wins Big
Interactive: Map to Victory
Issues: Republican Agenda
Gallery: Senate Leaders
This Issue: Table of Contents

TODAY ON TIME.com

• Best Inventions 2002
A foam-rubber microphone, a stealth surfboard, a genetically

Internet

Born Cassius Clay, Muhammad Ali is a native of Louisville, Kentucky.

woman to be elected governor of Kentucky. She was one of the first five women to be elected governor of a state.

Robert Penn Warren, the first poet laureate of the United States, was a Kentucky native. John James Audubon, a conservationist and nature artist, spent much of his life in the state. The John James Audubon Museum is in Henderson, Kentucky.

Country music stars from the state include Loretta Lynn, the Judd family, Billy Ray Cyrus, and Dwight Yoakam.

Other Kentucky celebrities include former world heavyweight boxing champion Muhammad Ali, Coach Adolph Rupp, Colonel Sanders, and Diane Sawyer. Ali was born in Louisville in 1942 as Cassius Clay. He won a gold medal at the 1960 Olympic Games and won the heavyweight title four years later. At about the same time, he converted to Islam and changed his name to Muhammad Ali. Rupp gained fame coaching basketball at the University of Kentucky for more than forty years. Colonel Harlan Sanders was the founder of the chain of Kentucky Fried Chicken restaurants, now called KFC. Television journalist Diane Sawyer was born in Glasgow,

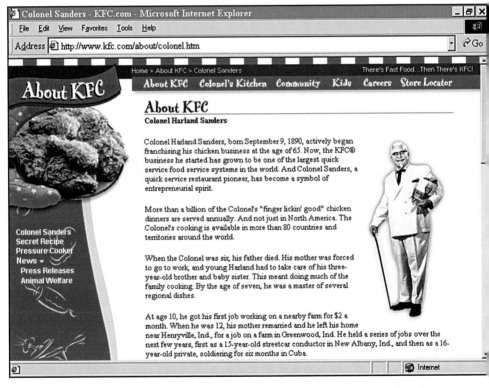

Colonel Sanders - KFC.com - Microsoft Internet Explorer

File   Edit   View   Favorites   Tools   Help

Address http://www.kfc.com/about/colonel.htm   Go

Home > About KFC > Colonel Sanders   There's Fast Food...Then There's KFC!

About KFC   Colonel's Kitchen   Community   Kids   Careers   Store Locator

About KFC

About KFC

Colonel Harland Sanders

Colonel Harland Sanders, born September 9, 1890, actively began franchising his chicken business at the age of 65. Now, the KFC® business he started has grown to be one of the largest quick service food service systems in the world. And Colonel Sanders, a quick service restaurant pioneer, has become a symbol of entrepreneurial spirit.

More than a billion of the Colonel's "finger lickin' good" chicken dinners are served annually. And not just in North America. The Colonel's cooking is available in more than 80 countries and territories around the world.

When the Colonel was six, his father died. His mother was forced to go to work, and young Harland had to take care of his three-year-old brother and baby sister. This meant doing much of the family cooking. By the age of seven, he was a master of several regional dishes.

At age 10, he got his first job working on a nearby farm for $2 a month. When he was 12, his mother remarried and he left his home near Henryville, Ind., for a job on a farm in Greenwood, Ind. He held a series of jobs over the next few years, first as a 15-year-old streetcar conductor in New Albany, Ind., and then as a 16-year-old private, soldiering for six months in Cuba.

Colonel Sanders
Secret Recipe
Pressure Cooker
News ▾
   Press Releases
   Animal Welfare

Internet

Colonel Harland Sanders began making his famous fried chicken for hungry travelers in Corbin, Kentucky. Now his recipe may be enjoyed by people all across the United States.

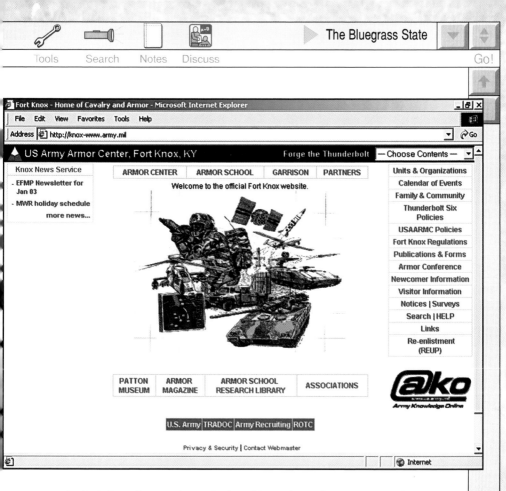

Fort Knox houses the nation's gold supply, and is an active military base. Visitors can also visit the Patton Museum.

Kentucky. Her first job after university was as a weather reporter in Louisville.

One last Kentucky celebrity is not a person but a building: Fort Knox, where the gold supply of the United States government is stored. Billions of dollars worth of gold is kept underground there and is carefully guarded. The Patton Museum of Cavalry and Armor is also located at Fort Knox. Visitors can view various armored vehicles, as well as some of General George S. Patton, Jr.'s, personal belongings.

Land and Climate

Kentucky is bordered on the north by Illinois, Indiana, and Ohio. West Virginia and Virginia lie to the east, Tennessee to the south, and Missouri to the west. The Ohio River runs along Kentucky's northern border, the Mississippi River marks the western boundary, and the Tug Fork River forms the border with West Virginia. The Appalachian Mountains are in the eastern part of the state. The western part of the state is in the low-lying Mississippi River Valley.

▶ Land of Contrasts

Kentucky has a wide variety of geographic regions and big differences in climate. The highest point is Black Mountain, at 4,145 feet above sea level. Black Mountain is in eastern Kentucky, the coolest and most mountainous part of the state. Kentucky's lowest point is on its western edge in the Mississippi Valley, just 78 feet above sea level.

The climate is generally warm and moist. In winter the average temperature is 35°F. In summer it rises to 77°F. The record low temperature in the state is –34°F, and the record high is 114°F. The state averages about fifty inches of rain a year. The eastern mountains receive about fifteen inches of snow each winter.

There are five major geographic regions in Kentucky. The Appalachian Plateau lies in the eastern part of the state and includes the state's biggest mountains. The Bluegrass region is in the north-central part of the state. This

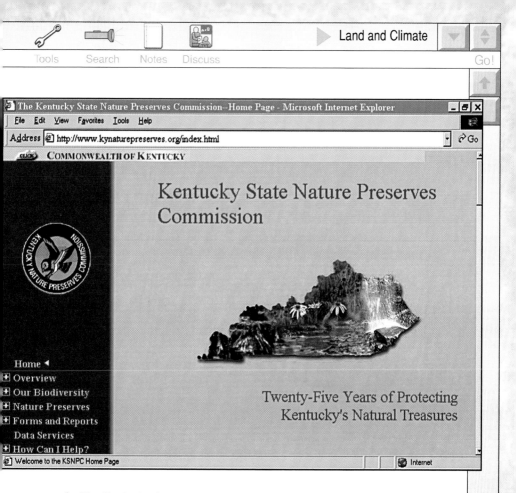

Kentucky State Nature Preserves Commission

Twenty-Five Years of Protecting
Kentucky's Natural Treasures

The Kentucky State Nature Preserves Commission works to protect the state's natural beauty. This includes over 650 animal, plant, and natural elements within Kentucky that are considered to be rare or are an endangered species.

area has gently-rolling plains, grazing fields, and the trademark bluegrass of Kentucky. Surprisingly, the bluegrass is not native to Kentucky. It was brought from England, probably in the late eighteenth century.

The Pennyroyal region in the south-central part of the state includes both the western part of the mountains and rolling plains similar to the Bluegrass region. The most interesting feature of the Pennyroyal is not immediately visible—vast caves formed by underground springs lie beneath the earth's surface. Mammoth Cave lies in the

Pennyroyal. It is the world's longest known cave system, connecting 348 miles of underground chambers and passages. Tourists from around the world visit the spectacular rock formations and hike on the outdoor trails of the surrounding park. The park has many underground lakes and rivers, including Echo River. Living in the underground darkness are eyeless fish; insects; shellfish; and other species that have adapted to this environment.

Deer, foxes, rabbits, raccoons, and other small mammals are found throughout the state.

The Western Coal Field region, named for its coal deposits, lies in northwestern Kentucky. Part of this area

▲ Mammoth Cave is one of Kentucky's best-known tourist attractions. With 348 miles of underground caverns, it is the longest known cave system.

contains limestone rock formations and caves. The Jackson Purchase region is the westernmost part of Kentucky. This section was added to the state about twenty-five years after Kentucky was admitted as a state in the Union, when Governor Isaac Shelby and General Andrew Jackson bought American Indian claims to the land. The Jackson Purchase includes marshes and lowlands along the Mississippi River, as well as some of Kentucky's largest bodies of water. Visitors come to this area in particular to fish for bluegills, walleyes, rockfish, and other species.

Most of Kentucky's population lives in the Bluegrass and Pennyroyal regions. The state's largest city is Lexington-Fayette, with a population of about 260,000. It is in the Bluegrass region. Also located in that region are the major cities of Covington and Frankfort, the state capital. Louisville, Owensboro, and Bowling Green are in the Pennyroyal region. Louisville has a population of more than 250,000 and was the state's largest city until the 2000 census. Hopkinsville and Henderson are the largest cities in the Western Coal Field. Ashland is the largest city in the Appalachian Plateau, and Paducah is the principal city within the Jackson Purchase. Paducah is an industrial and shipping center on the Ohio River.

The cardinal is Kentucky's state bird. It is the only bird that lives in the state all year long.

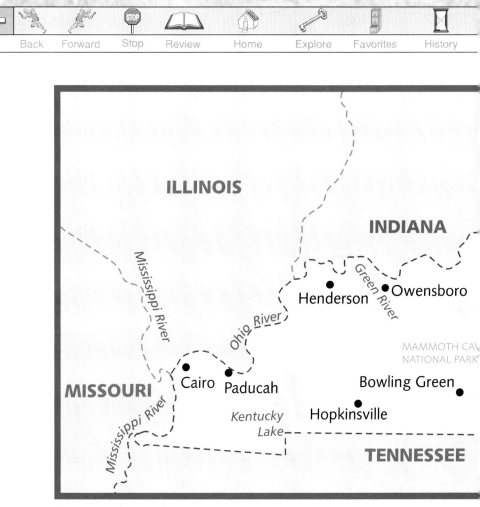

ILLINOIS

INDIANA

Mississippi River

Green River

Henderson ● Owensboro

Ohio River

MAMMOTH CA\
NATIONAL PARK

MISSOURI

● Cairo ● Paducah

Bowling Green ●

Kentucky Lake

Hopkinsville

Mississippi River

TENNESSEE

🔺 *A map of Kentucky.*

▷ Rivers and Falls

Rivers have played a major role in the development of Kentucky. The Ohio River runs more than 400 miles along the state's northern border. The Mississippi River borders Kentucky for about 50 miles. These two rivers were major routes in and out of Kentucky before the days of railroads and motor vehicles.

Rivers within Kentucky's borders include the Green, the Kentucky, and the Cumberland. Kentucky Lake and Cumberland Lake are the two biggest lakes in Kentucky.

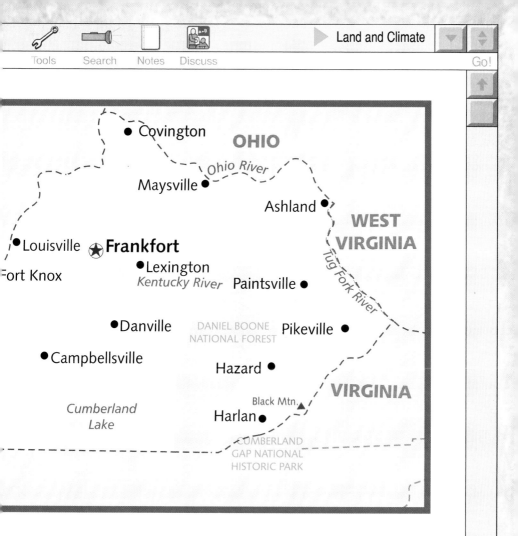

Cumberland Falls on the Cumberland River, 68 feet high, is one of the biggest waterfalls in the eastern United States.

A travel guide gives visitors a special reason to visit Cumberland Falls: "By night, when the moon is full and the sky clear, a mysterious moonbow appears in the mist. This is the only place in the Western Hemisphere where this phenomenon can be seen."[1] Moonbows are created in the same way as rainbows, except that moonlight shines through the water instead of sunlight.

Economy

Agriculture was the mainstay of Kentucky's economy until the twentieth century. Then, coal became readily available. In the 1940s, the arrival of low-cost hydroelectricity, attracted more industry.

Many of the businesses for which Kentucky is famous began early in the state's history. Distilling of bourbon whiskey started in the early nineteenth century. Kentucky produces more whiskey today than any other state. The soil and climate are especially suited to tobacco growing, and this also became a major industry in the nineteenth century. Other agricultural products include wheat, oats, hay, soybeans, and dairy goods.

Horse breeding and racing date back to Kentucky's earliest days. Coal mining emerged in the late nineteenth century and early twentieth century. Kentucky is still one of the country's major coal producers. Demand for coal has decreased in the twentieth century, but the energy crisis of the 1970s gave a boost to the industry.

Manufacturing, printing and publishing, and service industries, such as restaurants and tourism, round out Kentucky's economy.

▷ Strife and Struggle

Economic growth in Kentucky was occasionally accompanied by conflict and violence.

For many years, Kentucky was the United States' biggest producer of tobacco. Early in the twentieth century,

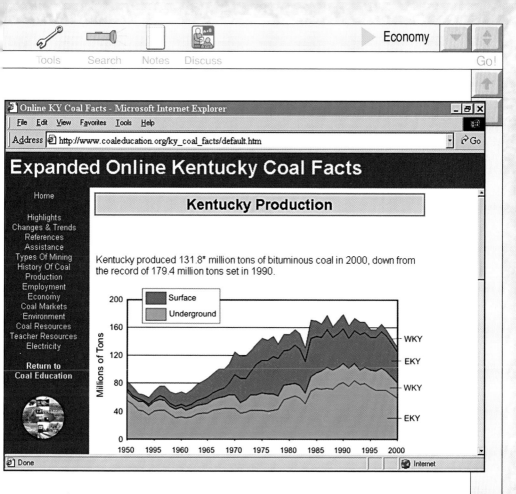

Expanded Online Kentucky Coal Facts

Home

Highlights
Changes & Trends
References
Assistance
Types Of Mining
History Of Coal
Production
Employment
Economy
Coal Markets
Environment
Coal Resources
Teacher Resources
Electricity

**Return to
Coal Education**

Kentucky Production

Kentucky produced 131.8* million tons of bituminous coal in 2000, down from the record of 179.4 million tons set in 1990.

Done   Internet

In 1820, the McLean drift bank, located near the Green River in Muhlenberg County, became the first commercial mine in Kentucky. The state's coal production peaked in 1990 when 179.4 million tons were extracted from the land.

major tobacco companies tried to keep the prices they paid to tobacco farmers at a low level. Farmers disagreed violently over whether to do business with the companies, and disputes between farmers left farms and tobacco fields destroyed. This conflict, which lasted from about 1903 to 1908, was known as the Black Patch War.

Tobacco use has declined in the last few decades. The product is now recognized as a health risk, and many Americans have given up the habit of smoking or chewing it.

Yet, tobacco is still Kentucky's most important agricultural crop. Kentucky remained the leading tobacco-producing state until the 1930s. Only North Carolina produces more.

Coal mining grew rapidly after the construction of railroads in Kentucky made transportation possible. World War I created even more demand for coal. As with tobacco, large companies tried to take total control of the coal industry in the state. Coal miners were poorly paid and worked under harsh and dangerous conditions. The economic problems of the Great Depression in the 1930s made life even harder. The miners tried to form unions to protect their rights and to seek higher wages. The coal companies refused to recognize these unions, and the "coal wars" resulted. The companies hired replacement workers and private police forces. The workers responded by destroying company property. Harlan County, a major coal-mining area, was known as "Bloody Harlan" because of the severe fighting that took place there.

Horse Power

Horse breeding and raising have become a hallmark of Kentucky farming. The first racehorses were actually workhorses. Their owners raced them against each other for entertainment. Wealthy Kentucky farmers soon began breeding and raising horses especially for racing and horse shows. At the Kentucky Horse Park and International Museum of the Horse, near Lexington, visitors can see exhibits about horses and riding, watch a variety of horse shows and events, and meet some retired champions.

Manufacturing

Another sports-related business with a long history in Kentucky is the making of baseball bats. Louisville

Sluggers, named for the Kentucky city, have been used by some of the game's most famous players.

Other products made in Kentucky include automobiles and transportation equipment, electrical equipment, chemicals, clothing, and packaged foods. Computer maker IBM opened a plant in Lexington in 1956, and other producers of computers and high-tech equipment have followed.

Tourism

Kentucky has made great efforts in recent decades to increase tourism. As a result, the money earned from tourism doubled between 1980 and 1990. Lincoln's birthplace and Daniel

http://memory.loc.gov/ammem/today/images/0607boone_big.jpg - Microsoft Internet Explorer

File   Edit   View   Favorites   Tools   Help

Address http://memory.loc.gov/ammem/today/images/0607boone_big.jpg

Done   Internet

▲ Frontiersman Daniel Boone was instrumental in settling present-day Kentucky.

Boone's early settlements are big attractions. Natural wonders such as the Daniel Boone National Forest, Cumberland Falls and the Cumberland River, and Mammoth Cave National Park offer a wide variety of outdoor activities. Riverboat rides on the Ohio and Mississippi rivers are also popular, as are visits to the original KFC restaurant in Corbin.

Education

The academic and basketball programs at the universities of Kentucky and Louisville are well known and attract students and fans from around the country. Both schools are known for their medical programs, and the University of Kentucky is also strong in agriculture.

Transylvania University was founded in 1780 during the early frontier days. It is highly regarded as a liberal arts

The Memorial Building at Lincoln's birthplace is located on the Sinking Spring Farm in Hodgenville, Kentucky.

△ Originally named Agricultural and Mechanical College, the University of Kentucky was renamed in 1816. It is located in Lexington, Kentucky.

college. Berea College was one of the first colleges where whites and African Americans attended classes together. It is known for its work-study program. Students must work between ten and fifteen hours a week in approved jobs on the campus and in the community.

Government

Kentucky was admitted to the union in 1792 as the fifteenth state. Before that, it had been a county of Virginia, and then a separate territory.

▷ Kentucky's Constitution

Kentucky's first constitution went into effect when it became a state. The state is now governed according to its fourth constitution, which was enacted in 1891.

Amendments to the constitution must be approved by at least three fifths of the members of the state's legislature, and then by the voters in a statewide election. The constitution can also be amended through a constitutional convention.

▷ Structure of Government

Like most states and the federal government, Kentucky's government is divided into three branches: executive, legislative, and judicial. The chief executive is the governor. Other members of the executive branch are the lieutenant governor, attorney general, secretary of state, and treasurer. These officials are elected to four-year terms with a two-term limit.

The legislature, or law-making body, consists of a house of representatives and a senate. Representatives are elected for two-year terms while senators are elected every four years.

The Kentucky Supreme Court heads the judicial branch. This court has seven members, each representing a

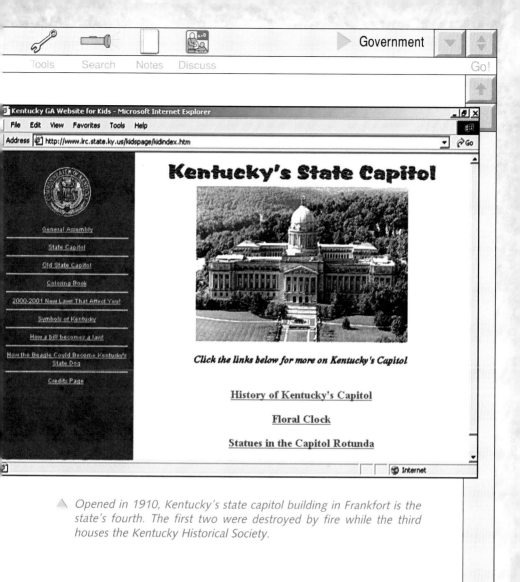

Kentucky's State Capitol

General Assembly

State Capitol

Old State Capitol

Coloring Book

2000-2001 New Laws That Affect You!

Symbols of Kentucky

How a bill becomes a law!

How the Beagle Could Become Kentucky's State Dog

Credits Page

Click the links below for more on Kentucky's Capitol

History of Kentucky's Capitol

Floral Clock

Statues in the Capitol Rotunda

Opened in 1910, Kentucky's state capitol building in Frankfort is the state's fourth. The first two were destroyed by fire while the third houses the Kentucky Historical Society.

different part of the state. Below the supreme court are a court of appeals, circuit courts, and district courts. Judges are elected to the supreme court, court of appeals, and circuit courts for terms of eight years and to district courts for four-year terms.

County government is also important in Kentucky, which has 120 counties. That is more than any other state except Texas and Georgia. The county judge is the chief executive in county government. He or she is assisted by justices of the peace or commissioners. During much of

Georgia Davis Powers

When Georgia Davis Powers took her seat in the General Assembly in 1968, she represented two "firsts": the first African American and the first woman ever elected to the Kentucky Senate. She became a champion of civil rights and special education.

Living the Story > Gallery > Photo 16

Internet

In 1968, Georgia David Powers became the first woman, as well as the first African American, to be elected to the Kentucky State Senate.

Kentucky's history, county governments were actually more powerful in some areas than the state government. This resulted in widespread abuse of power by local officials. The constitution of 1891 limited the powers of county government. Still, county governments in Kentucky continue to make decisions on some major issues.

History

Nomadic hunters known as Paleo-Indians were present in Kentucky as long as ten thousand years ago. During the Adena era, about three thousand years ago, the descendants of these people built massive burial mounds. The mounds indicate that their society was highly advanced for its time. Some early explorers wondered if a lost race or biblical tribe had once lived in North America.

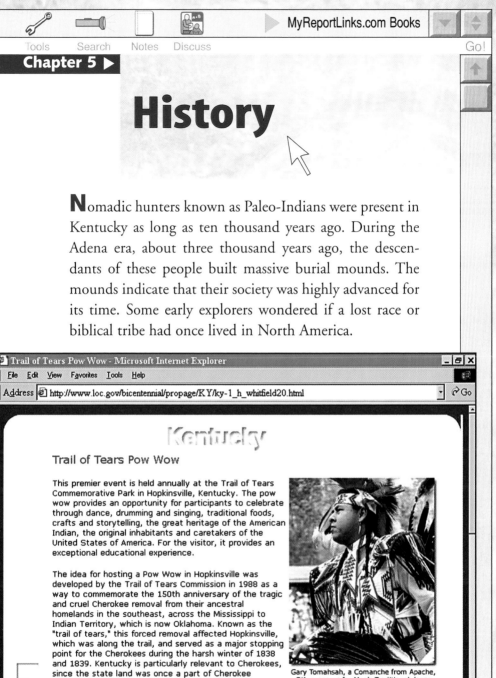

Trail of Tears Pow Wow - Microsoft Internet Explorer

File   Edit   View   Favorites   Tools   Help

Address 🗐 http://www.loc.gov/bicentennial/propage/KY/ky-1_h_whitfield20.html   ↗ Go

Kentucky

Trail of Tears Pow Wow

This premier event is held annually at the Trail of Tears Commemorative Park in Hopkinsville, Kentucky. The pow wow provides an opportunity for participants to celebrate through dance, drumming and singing, traditional foods, crafts and storytelling, the great heritage of the American Indian, the original inhabitants and caretakers of the United States of America. For the visitor, it provides an exceptional educational experience.

The idea for hosting a Pow Wow in Hopkinsville was developed by the Trail of Tears Commission in 1988 as a way to commemorate the 150th anniversary of the tragic and cruel Cherokee removal from their ancestral homelands in the southeast, across the Mississippi to Indian Territory, which is now Oklahoma. Known as the "trail of tears," this forced removal affected Hopkinsville, which was along the trail, and served as a major stopping point for the Cherokees during the harsh winter of 1838 and 1839. Kentucky is particularly relevant to Cherokees, since the state land was once a part of Cherokee ancestral homeland.

Gary Tomahsah, a Comanche from Apache, OK, prepares for Men's Traditional dance competition at 1999 Pow Wow
Photo: Midge Durbin

The president and founder of the Trail of Tears

🗐 Done   🌐 Internet

▲ Held at the Trail of Tears Commemorative Park in Hopkinsville, Kentucky, each year since 1989, the Trail of Tears Pow Wow features costumed dance competitions and crafts demonstrations.

▶ Conflicts with Settlers

By the time the first explorers arrived, however, there were few American Indians left in Kentucky. This may have been the result of fighting among the tribes or of diseases introduced by the Europeans. The native inhabitants are believed to have called the region "dark and bloody ground" because of the number of deaths there.

The American Indians who remained did not welcome the newcomers. Clashes broke out between the Europeans and the tribes that used Kentucky territory as their hunting grounds. The American Indians often seized furs, skins, and other goods taken from the area by the Europeans. Later, the American Indians went so far as to capture and kill white explorers and settlers in Kentucky. This problem grew during the Revolutionary War (1775–83), when the British encouraged the American Indians to attack the new settlers.

After the colonists won the Revolutionary War, the British stopped supporting the American Indians. This led to a great reduction in the threat of attack.

▶ First Settlers and Explorers

French explorers were the first Europeans to see Kentucky. In the late seventeenth century, René-Robert Cavelier, Sieur de La Salle, claimed the entire Mississippi Valley for France. However, it was not until after the French and Indian War (1754–63) that Europeans began settling in Kentucky on a permanent basis. At that point, Britain still had control of American territory east of the Mississippi.

Two pioneers—John Findley of Pennsylvania and Thomas Walker of Virginia—blazed separate trails that many would follow into Kentucky. Findley came down the

Ohio River. In 1750, Walker discovered an opening through the rugged mountains at the southeast corner of Kentucky. This passage was called the Cumberland Gap. It would become the main route into Kentucky. Among those who used this route were a group of men called long hunters, because they spent long periods hunting in the woods. The most famous long hunter was Daniel Boone.

▷ Legend and Reality

Daniel Boone moved his family to Kentucky in 1775 after spending time exploring the region. He established a trail called the Wilderness Road that took many colonists

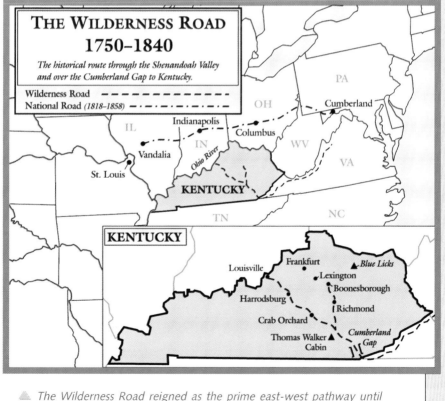

The Wilderness Road reigned as the prime east-west pathway until the wider, smoother National Road opened in the early 1800s.

through the Cumberland Gap into Kentucky. He built a fort and stockade at Boonesborough, which is now a national park. During his time on the frontier, Boone had many exciting adventures. Although he usually lived peacefully with the American Indians, fights sometimes developed. He was captured at least twice.

These exciting experiences became a favorite subject for writers and storytellers in the late eighteenth and nineteenth centuries. These popular stories often contained exaggerations and even lies about Boone's activities. Even when the stories were true, they made Boone sound like a superhero. These tales became very popular in the United States and elsewhere in the world and made Boone a legendary figure.

At Boone's funeral in 1820, long-time friend John Coburn said that Boone had been "the instrument of opening the road to millions of the human family from the pressure of sterility and want, to a land flowing with milk and honey."[1] Boone's trailblazing gave people the hope that they would have a better future in a new land.

Hostility Toward Britain

Daniel Boone's leadership helped Kentucky to grow rapidly. Between 1780 and 1790, the population went from just a few hundred to nearly one hundred thousand. At that time, Kentucky was a county of Virginia. The settlers moving into the area asked for statehood, and this was granted in 1792. Kentucky became the first state west of the Appalachians. By 1820, there were more than half a million people in Kentucky, making it the sixth-largest state in the nation. Kentucky was to play an important role in shaping the nation's history during much of the nineteenth century.

Henry Clay served as a Kentucky statesman for nearly fifty years. Known as the Great Compromiser, he managed to negotiate several agreements between the North and the South in the years leading up to the Civil War. These agreements included the Compromise of 1850, which allowed slavery in the New Mexico and Utah territories but prohibited it in California.

Anti-British feelings remained strong on the frontier. Many settlers believed Britain was encouraging the American Indians to attack settlers. Henry Clay (1777–1852) was a nationally known statesman who represented Kentucky both in the U.S. House of Representatives and the Senate for much of the first half of the nineteenth century. Clay's hostility to the British and his support for war against Great Britain were important in persuading the United States government to enter the War of 1812. In fact, many people came to refer to it as "Mr. Clay's War."

The Civil War

The issues of slavery and civil rights were major sources of disagreement in Kentucky. There was heated debate over whether to allow slavery when the state was formed. In the end, slavery was permitted by the first state constitution.

Henry Clay was prominent in events leading up to the Civil War. Clay favored abolition of slavery, but wanted to go about it slowly. As a congressional leader, Clay worked to help people on different sides of the issue to see each other's point of view. The compromises that he obtained

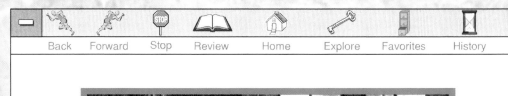

△ Kentucky native Abe Lincoln surrounded himself with his closest advisors during the Civil War years. Seated from left to right are Major General William T. Sherman, Major General Ulysses S. Grant, President Abraham Lincoln, and Admiral David Dixon Porter.

were important in delaying the start of the Civil War until the 1860s.

When war eventually came, Kentucky chose at first to stay neutral. Both the Union and the Confederacy wanted to win Kentucky over to their side. Kentucky's central location, its large population, and its numerous resources made it attractive. President Lincoln is often quoted as saying, "I hope to have God on my side, but I must have Kentucky."[2]

Kentucky later declared its support for the Union, although some Kentuckians formed a rival government and declared themselves loyal to the Confederacy.

People throughout Kentucky were bitterly divided and took different sides during the war, which lasted from 1861 to 1865. Kentuckians served in both armies, and both sides included a star for Kentucky on their flags.

Kentuckian John Cabell Breckinridge was vice president of the United States from 1857 to 1861. Unlike Clay, Breckinridge favored the continuation of slavery. During the Civil War, he joined the Confederacy and became a general in the Confederate Army. Toward the end of the war, he was the Confederate secretary of war.

A major battle between Confederate and Union forces took place in the central Kentucky town of Perryville in October 1862. This battle ended in a draw, but the Confederate troops were forced to withdraw from Kentucky. The Union Army therefore gained control over the strategically-important state.

Once the war was over, differences of opinion about slavery and civil rights would continue to cause conflict in Kentucky for many years to come.

Continuing Strife

After the war, Kentucky passed laws to protect the rights of newly-freed slaves. However these laws were poorly enforced, and feelings for and against slavery were still strong. This led to troubled race relations and violence against African Americans. Many African Americans' homes and property were destroyed, and more than one hundred died in lynchings.

John Cabell Breckinridge was a former U.S. vice president. During the Civil War, he sided with the Confederates.

Yet racial conflict was not Kentucky's only problem following the Civil War.

Two families, the Hatfields and the McCoys, became famous for their family feud. It lasted ten years and resulted in the deaths of a dozen family members. The feud was widely reported and created an image that Kentucky residents were backward and ignorant.

In 1899, disputes erupted over an election for governor. The candidates were Democrat William Goebel and Republican William Taylor. Stephen Channing describes how violent the campaign became. "Week after campaign week, the atmosphere of distrust grew. Friends became bitter enemies; claims of fraud and deceit, warnings of retribution, and death threats filled the air. Election day itself was marred by the deaths of fifteen men killed at various polling places around the state . . ."[3]

The first results showed Taylor winning by a very narrow margin. The Democrats, who controlled the state legislature, challenged these results. It seemed likely that they would say the voting had been unfair and that Goebel was the winner. Before they announced their decision, Goebel was shot. The Democratic legislators declared Goebel the legally-elected governor just before he died. Republicans continued to recognize Taylor as the winner. The dispute was not settled until May 1900, when the U.S. Supreme Court agreed with the Democrats. In the meantime, Republicans and Democrats operated two entirely separate governments in Kentucky.

In the decades that followed, there were violent conflicts within the tobacco and coal industries. The strong growth that Kentucky had experienced well into the nineteenth century slowed after the Civil War. Kentucky lagged behind many other states in productivity and income levels. Education and public services suffered from a lack of resources and attention.

Twentieth-Century Reforms

With such a history of turmoil behind them, many Kentuckians wanted to improve conditions in their state.

🔺 *Louisville is one of Kentucky's largest cities and home to the Kentucky Derby, one of the longest continuously-run horse races in the United States.*

Some progress was made after the election of Albert Benjamin "Happy" Chandler as governor in 1935. Chandler's reforms followed the federal programs started during the New Deal of President Franklin D. Roosevelt. Chandler passed laws to provide pensions for the elderly and to restrict child labor.

Other elected officials continued to make efforts to improve the state's economy and end unfair race practices. Kentucky also followed the federal government's lead on racial integration. In the late 1940s, Kentucky acted to provide equality in its state universities. In 1954, the U.S. Supreme Court ruled that segregated schools were illegal.

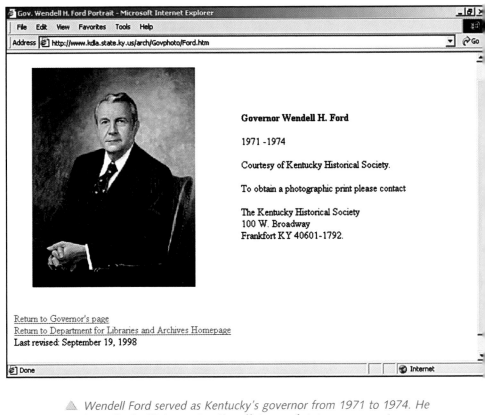

⚠ Wendell Ford served as Kentucky's governor from 1971 to 1974. He is credited with improving the efficiency of state government.

Kentucky was more successful than most Southern states in integrating its public schools. Even some large northern cities experienced more difficulty in trying to make education equally available for people of all races.

In the 1960s, Governor Bert Combs greatly increased public money for education and other social services. Then in the 1970s, Governor Wendell Ford reduced the size of the state government and improved its efficiency. The state legislature passed laws to ensure working and housing rights for minorities. Civil rights laws passed in Kentucky in the mid-twentieth century were noted and praised by people throughout the nation.

In the late 1960s, Kentucky passed civil rights laws that went further than any other state laws in the nation in protecting people against discrimination in job hiring and housing.

Recent History

The 1970s was a decade of growth for the coal-mining area around Lexington, Kentucky. An energy shortage in the United States during the 1970s, caused people to seek out Kentucky's coal resources. The economy boomed, but the process of strip-mining the land to get the coal was harming the environment. Eventually a law was passed requiring owners of strip mines to restore the land after they were done mining it.

The automobile industry came to Kentucky in the late 1980s. The Toyota Motor Manufacturing company opened a plant in Georgetown, Kentucky, located just north of Lexington. As a result, dozens of plants that manufacture car parts opened up throughout the state.

Toyota Company President Shoichiro Toyoda spoke at the factory opening. He said that the plant represented,

▲ *The state of Kentucky promotes tourism. This photo shows a family on an outing to the Boone Trace Hiking Trail.*

"a spirit of successfully merging the manufacturing ideals and practices of two nations in order to build a new tradition of success."[4]

Education continued to be a top priority. In 1989, the Kentucky Supreme Court took major action toward improving the state's schools. It ruled that the state's public education system did not provide equal opportunities to all students. In response to this, lawmakers passed the Kentucky Education Reform Act. This law proved to be effective. Before it became law, Kentucky had ranked at or near the bottom among the states in student performance, number of high school graduates, and amount of money spent per student. Only five years later, the National Education Association rated Kentucky schools among the top three states.

Improvements in civil rights and living and working conditions have helped to make Kentucky a better place. Kentucky's government has also made efforts to attract new, modern businesses to the state. Steps have been taken to improve the state's environment and clean up pollution. Tourism and travel within Kentucky are being promoted.

Kentucky's people look upon their state's recent achievements with pride. The possibility of a brighter future in Kentucky seems stronger now than at any time since when the state was seen as the gateway to a promised land in the distant western frontier. As famous novelist Jesse Stuart once wrote, "Kentucky is neither southern, northern, eastern, western, it is the core of America. If these United States can be called a body Kentucky is its heart."[5]

Chapter 1. The Bluegrass State

1. Stephen A. Channing, *Kentucky: A Bicentennial History* (New York: W. W. Norton and Company, 1977), p. 4.

Chapter 2. Land and Climate

1. *Mobil Travel Guide Southeast 2001* (Lincolnwood, IL: Publications International, 2001), p. 259.

Chapter 5. History

1. As quoted in John Mack Faragher, *Daniel Boone: The Life and Legend of an American Pioneer* (New York: Henry Holt and Company, 1992), p. 322.

2. Abraham Lincoln as quoted by Mark Coomes, "Battle of Perryville Reenactment is Logistical Challenge," *The Louisville Scene*, October 1, 2002, <http://www.louisvillescene.com/calendar/features/2002/20021001perryville.html> (November 15, 2002).

3. Stephen A. Channing, *Kentucky: A Bicentennial History* (New York: W. W. Norton and Company, 1977), p. 170.

4. Quoted in "Toyota Celebrates Dedication of $800 Million Kentucky Plant," Public Relations Newswire, October 6, 1988.

5. Jesse Stuart, as quoted by Kentucky Tourism Council, "tourky.com," *Kentucky Tourism Council*, 2002, <http://www.tourky.com> (January 7, 2003).

Further Reading

Aylesworth, Thomas G. and Virginia L. *The Southeast: Georgia, Kentucky, Tennessee*. State Reports Series. New York: Chelsea House Publishers, 1991.

Barret, Tracey. *Kentucky*. Tarrytown, N.Y.: Benchmark Books/Marshall Cavendish, 1999.

Green, Carol. *Daniel Boone: Man of the Forests*. Chicago: Children's Press, 1990.

Kavanagh, James. *Kentucky Birds*. Blaine, Wash.: Waterford Press, 1999.

Lynn, Loretta, with George Vecsey. *Coal Miner's Daughter*. New York: Da Capo Press, 2001.

Loeper, John J. *Meet the Drakes on the Kentucky Frontier*. Tarrytown, NY: Benchmark Books/Marshall Cavendish, 1999.

Marsh, Carole. *The Kentucky Experience Pocket Guide*. Peachtree City, Ga.: Gallopede International, 2000.

Smith, Adam and Katherine S. *A Historical Album of Kentucky*. Brookfield, Conn.: Millbrook Press, Inc., 1995.

Stein, R. Conrad. *Kentucky*. Danbury, Conn.: Children's Press, 1999.

Thompson, Kathleen. *Kentucky*. Austin, Tex.: Raintree Steck-Vaughn Publishers, 1996.

Williams, Suzanne M. *Kentucky*. Danbury, Conn.: Children's Press, 2001.